Beyond Ourselves

A course which explores the wider meaning
of our lives

Member's Course book

Beyond Ourselves is Book 1 of *The God Who Is There*
the ReSource discipleship course for small groups

ReSource

Published by:
ReSource
13 Sadler Street, Wells, Somerset BA5 2RR
office@resource-arm.net
www.resource-arm.net
Charity no. 327035

ISBN 978-1-906363-31-4

Cover image © iStockphoto.com
Cover photograph © Alison Morgan
Images on pp 9,14,17,19,23,24,29,37,40,42,44,49,53,54,55 ©
iStockphoto.com
Image on p 16 ©stockxpert.com
Image on pp 8,18,51 © 123RF.com
Image on pp 10,12,21,28,33,35,47,61,64,66,74 © Fotolia.co.uk
Images on pp 11,41 © Microsoft

This course is edited by Roger Morgan, working with Anita Benson. We are
grateful to the following people who have contributed to the writing of
the individual sessions: John Benson, Ian Bishop, Pete Greaves, Mike
Harrison, Alison Morgan, Richard Morgan, Michael Selman, Karin Silk,
Elaine Sutherland, Lauren Wicks, and Angela Zvespar.

Beyond Ourselves

Contents

Preface

Welcome to the new ReSource series on discipleship, which we have entitled *The God Who is There.* At present three books are planned in the series; each book provides a course of ten sessions suitable for small groups. This book, *Beyond Ourselves*, asks the question 'Is there anything beyond ourselves?' or in other words 'Is God there?'. By the end of the course the course members should be able to say 'Yes – I am sure God is there, because I have experienced him for myself.' The second book, *The New Community*, is about continuing to find God to be there whenever a group of Christians meet and search for him together. The third book, *Shining Like Stars*, is about finding God to be there in ordinary day to day life.

The God Who is There takes its inspiration from *Rooted in Jesus,* a discipleship course written ten years ago for rural Africa. *Rooted in Jesus* has been highly successful, having been translated so far into 27 African languages and adopted in 13 countries. It has been used to transform many lives as well as whole churches and communities. Because of its success in Africa many people have asked us to release *Rooted in Jesus* for use in the West, believing, as we do, that discipleship is needed here too.

The God Who is There series is our response to that request. *The God Who is There* has the same aims and a similar style to *Rooted in Jesus,* and also has much overlapping content. At first we thought we could keep the same structure and chapter headings and just make a few revisions, but we found that this did not work and decided to do a complete rewrite. The illustrations and examples used in the two series have had to be very different because the issues and problems westerners face in their daily lives are mostly quite different from those people face in Africa. And in *The God Who is There* we have tried to relate to western moral and philosophical assumptions. For example, to most people in rural Africa it is obvious that God is there. But in the West to live by faith in God is to live in a way that stands out from the norm.

For each of the three courses in the series there is a Leader's Manual and an accompanying Coursebook for each group member. Books 2 and 3 also involve music, and come with a worship CD. The series is suitable for groups of any size. It will work well with just three people, but it could equally well be used by a large church with many groups meeting together at the same time.

The series was written by a team of contributors and edited by Roger Morgan and Anita Benson. Roger and Anita and their team are able to offer training to churches or to group leaders. If you would like to find out how we can support you, please do get in touch with us by emailing office@resource-arm.net or calling 01749 672860. Or visit our websites, www.resource-arm.net and www.rootedinjesus.net.

Additional resources

If you enjoy this course and decide that you would like to pray a prayer of commitment to Christ, you may like to get hold of *Decision: an explanation of what is involved in becoming a Christian. Decision* is a short and inexpensive booklet which summarises the steps on the road to faith and explains what to expect next. It contains the stories of others who have made this journey, and will help remind you what it is that you have decided to do. *Decision* is available from the ReSource website or from your group leader.

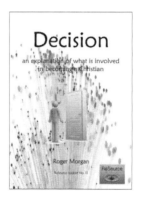

Beyond Ourselves

Session 1: God, creation, and me

Summary of the session

Many people have had experiences which lead them to the conclusion that there is something 'Beyond Ourselves' and many people look to the Bible as a way of interpreting those experiences.

The writers of the Bible looked at the world in which they lived and concluded that there must be a designer, whom they then called God. They believed it was natural to reach out to God and to search for him.

The assumption that the universe has a designer is questioned today by some scientists and philosophers. Indeed some scientists are atheists; but in fact atheism goes further than the scientific evidence allows. It requires faith to be an atheist, and in practice it is (and always has been) a philosophy adopted by a very small minority of people.

The universe is undoubtedly awesome and beautiful. If God exists he too must be awesome and beautiful. He must also be all seeing and all knowing.

According to the Bible, human beings are the culmination of God's design in creation. Each individual person has been designed by God to be exactly who they are, and each is known and loved by God. Our purpose is to discover the potential within us and in so doing to move closer to God.

Key verse

We encourage you to commit the key verse to memory each week; you will benefit greatly from it if you do!

Psalm 23.6 – 'Surely goodness and mercy shall follow me all the days of my life, and I shall dwell in the house of the Lord my whole life long.'

Needed during Session 1

At the beginning of Session 1 you will be asked to answer the following question: Have you ever experienced any of the following?

- A sense of the close presence of God or Jesus
- Answers to prayer
- The presence of evil
- Ghosts
- The presence of a person who is known to be dead
- Auras surrounding other people
- Supernatural protection or guidance
- Strange dreams or visions
- Speaking in tongues
- Supernatural healings
- Out-of-body experiences

Exercises following Session 1

Please complete one of these four exercises before you come to the next session; choose whichever one seems best for you. If you have time, you may wish to complete all four. The first three are aimed at helping you to explore what you learned in the first session. The fourth is a preparation for the next session.

Exercise 1 – Psalm 23.6

Each day, before you go to sleep, think carefully about the key verse, **Psalm 23.6**. These words were written by David, the boy shepherd who became king in Jerusalem nearly three thousand years ago.

Ask yourself 'Did David know something that I do not know?' David believed that good things were happening to him all the time and that this was because the God who created him was caring for him. So ask yourself 'Is it possible that David's understanding of his life is the correct one? Can I imagine myself starting to think like this?'

Think about the day that is now ending. First spend at least five minutes making a list of all the good things that have happened today, most of them probably quite little things. Ask yourself 'Why did these good things happen to me? Is it possible that good things are going to happen to me day after day for the rest of my life and even beyond my life?'

Next think about the things that you got wrong today; things you did that you regret, things you said, things you thought. Is it possible, as David thought, that mercy could follow you as well as goodness? Is it possible that God knows your weaknesses and understands, even smiles, on them? Is it possible that all the bad things in your life could be forgiven and forgotten?

Now make a list of the unpleasant things that happened today. Is it possible, do you think, that even these things have been allowed to happen to you for a good purpose? What do you think that good purpose could be?

In the morning when you wake up, think about the day ahead. David went into every day assuming that God would watch over him. And so he would pray and ask for good things to happen that day. If this is a step you feel you could make, try praying about the day ahead, asking God to reveal to you his goodness and mercy today.

Finally David says that he believes that he will dwell in the house of God his whole life long. Imagine a safe place where you could always go, a place that could not be taken away from you, a place of peace and safety and blessing. If you believed that there was such a place and it was yours, what difference would this make to the way you live now?

Exercise 2 – Is there a designer?

William Paley is famous for his illustration about the watch and the watchmaker. He imagines himself finding a watch and examining it. He realises at once that this watch did not just happen, because it is clear that the watch has been designed: there must be a watchmaker. In the same way, argued Paley, anyone who looks at the universe cannot fail to conclude that it has a creator or designer.

St Paul said much the same thing, though in a much less scientific way. In **Romans 1.20** Paul wrote these words: 'Ever since the creation of the world his eternal power and divine nature, invisible though they are, have been understood and seen through the things he has made.'

Both Paley and Paul are inviting you to look around you. The existence of God is obvious, they suggest. Try looking at the world through their eyes. Can you see why they said what they did?

When Paul wrote 2000 years ago he followed the scientific assumptions of his day. He knew nothing about gravity or chemistry or electro-magnetism or evolution. Since then science has moved on and we now look at the world in a completely different way. Paley's ideas are more recent, but even so we know much more now than he did then. In 2000 more years science will have moved on again. That's how science works.

Here are some of the things which most scientists today seem to agree about. These are not things we can see with our eyes, like a peacock's tail or a beautiful sunset. But they are nevertheless awesome. Think about these things and reflect just how awesome they are. Do they lead you to agree with Paley and Paul? Does it seem to you, as it did to them, that the existence of a designer is more likely than that the universe as we observe it is the result of blind impersonal forces?

- The universe in which we live came into existence about 13.7 billion years ago. Scientists have no idea how or why except that there was some kind of explosive event which we call 'The Big Bang'. No one has any idea what came before the 'big bang'.

- Since then the universe has been expanding rapidly. There are now literally billions of stars like our sun, and billions of planets like the one we live on. As far as we know there is life on only one of these planets.

- The universe is held together by a force which we call gravity. From the beginning the size of this force was fixed. If the force of gravity was not exactly as it is, nothing in the universe would hold together.

- Another vital force in the universe is the force of magnetism. This also is fixed. If the ratio of the force of gravity to the force of magnetism was changed even by a tiny amount the universe would not work.

- The earth tilts at 23.5 degrees. It tilts at this angle because of the size and position of our moon, which got to that position as the result of a cosmic accident. A little less tilt, or a little more, and any kind of life on earth would be impossible.

- Life appeared on earth in primitive form about 5 billion years ago. Scientists have no idea how or why. So far, life has only ever been found on earth. Life here is only possible because of the precise distance between the earth and the sun.

- When life began on earth it took the form of a single cell which was capable of reproduction. Even this first cell was extremely complex and contained a vast amount of information. Life is passed on through an intricate and extremely complex mechanism called DNA.

- A human body has billions of cells, each of which contains billions of pieces of information – all of which is passed on at reproduction.

- Human beings have evolved over the centuries in a way that enabled them to adapt to their environment. The same is true for every species. Scientists speculate that one species can evolve into another but there is no clear evidence which proves this. The origin of each new species may be the result of a mechanistic process but each new species has the appearance of a miracle.

What do you think? Is our universe designed or did it just happen?

Exercise 3 – Being creative

Make something – it could be a meal, a painting, an object, a poem or even just writing a letter – anything that did not exist until you created it.

Before you begin your work of creation, look at **Psalm 139.14.** The Psalmist believed that everything in creation has been made by God very carefully. He believes that God has made him 'fearfully', making sure that he got nothing wrong, and 'wonderfully', regarding the outcome as amazing, something to be proud of, to cherish.

So when you create something, make it as you have made nothing before. Do it very carefully; realise that in so far as it is possible the thing that you have made is perfect, the best that it could be, the best you have ever done. And when you have finished, look at your work with pride, and be amazed that you could have made something so beautiful which just 24 hours ago did not exist at all.

Then sit for a while in front of a mirror. Ask yourself if it is possible that this is how God thinks about you?

If you can, bring whatever you have made to the group and ask if you can show it to the others.

Exercise 4 – Preparation for Session 2

In this first session, we have thought about how perfectly God has made us. Next time we will try to understand one of the profoundest questions of all, the question 'What is wrong?' Why is it that this beautiful world, so beautiful that it sometimes seems perfect, is after all flawed? And why am I flawed as a human being?

Think now about creation. In what ways is the created world flawed? In what ways does the world cause people to suffer? Ask yourself why this is? If God exists, what is he doing about it? Now consider **Isaiah**

65.17–25, which predicts that one day God plans to create a new world which is not flawed in the way that our world is.

Then think about yourself. In what ways are you flawed as a human being? Are you diseased, emotionally fragile, physically weak, confused in your mind, limited in your understanding…? What do you think about yourself?

Think also about the moral dimension. You know the difference between right and wrong; but is there a moral flaw in you, so that you are always doing what you know to be wrong? Imagine that since you were born a record has been kept – a record of all the bad things that you have done, said, or thought. Imagine that you were to die tonight and that the first thing that would happen after your death would be the revealing of that record. Think: 'What are three things that I have done that I would be most afraid to have revealed?' Then read **Hebrews 4.13** and **2 Corinthians 5.17**.

Beyond Ourselves

Session 2: What's wrong with the world?

Summary of the session

The world, despite its beauty and its wonder, contains much that is flawed. Suffering, death, sin, and injustice are plain for all to see. Those who believe in a God of love must offer an explanation for this.

It is plain that much of the suffering and injustice of this world is directly caused by the wrong way in which people choose to behave towards each other. The word the Bible uses for this wrong behaviour is sin. The Bible defines sin as breaking the law of God, and says that every human being who has ever lived has been guilty of sin at least to some degree. It is sin which spoils human relationships.

Sin also spoils the relationship between people and God. Because of sin we find ourselves alone, separated from God. Because we sin, God disciplines us and so it is that we all die and we all suffer.

This is all explained in the Bible through the story of Adam and Eve. Some Christians believe this story to be a historical account, but most Christians would say that this profound story should be read as you might look at a great picture. This story speaks to us about our own lives and about the human condition.

The Bible gives four explanations for suffering. Some suffering is caused directly by other people. Some suffering is caused by God's discipline. Some suffering is caused by the activity of an evil unseen spiritual force called Satan. And some suffering is allowed by God to test us.

There is no doubt that suffering, patiently borne, has good consequences. If death is the end, then suffering is bad because it is often unjust, but if death is not the end then suffering may be the best possible preparation for the next life.

Key verse

This week's verse is **Romans 6.23** – 'For the wages of sin is death, but the free gift of God is eternal life in Christ Jesus our Lord.'

Exercises following Session 2

Please complete one of these four exercises before you come to the next session; choose whichever one seems best for you. If you have time, you may wish to complete all four. The first three are aimed at helping you to explore what you learned in the first session. The fourth is a preparation for the next session.

Exercise 1 – Put things right

In the session we saw how wrongdoing can spoil relationships. Begin this exercise by thinking of someone with whom you know you have a bad relationship. Choose one person only – another day you can repeat the exercise with a second person in mind.

First try to decide whether wrongdoing is the cause of the bad relationship. Has either of you behaved badly towards the other, or is there another cause? If you believe the problem is your own poor behaviour, the wise thing is to go to the other person, say sorry for what you said or did, and ask them to forgive you. This takes courage, but it nearly always restores the relationship. Once in a while you will find the other person will not forgive – this is sad, but there is nothing that you can do about it. When asking forgiveness it is sometimes wise to take a small gift to help make it clear that you take responsibility and want to make amends.

If you feel the other person is at fault, the first step is to acknowledge your anger to yourself – it is never wrong and always healthy to feel angry when you have been badly treated. The second step is always to forgive the other person.

Forgiving someone is a deliberate letting go of your anger against them. One way to do this is to say a prayer, saying something like this: 'Father God, please forgive John for his behaviour. I do not want you to hold his behaviour against him. Instead, please bless him and help him. Thank you that Jesus died for John as he died for me and that Jesus wants us both to be forgiven.'

Sometimes after you have forgiven someone it is also wise to go and speak to them. You will have to decide whether or not to do this. If you do go, remember that your purpose is to make peace not war. So when you raise the matter with the other person always use sentences beginning with 'I' and not sentences beginning with 'you'. For example, 'John, I felt upset by what you said the other day and wondered if we could talk about it?' Do not say 'John you were very rude to me the other day and I have come to ask for an apology.'

Sometimes bad relationships are caused partly by your behaviour and partly by the other person's. In such cases, start by admitting your own fault and asking for forgiveness. This will often result in the other person doing the same.

Another common cause of a bad relationship is simply that each of you sees the same issue from a different point of view. Such conflicts are not resolved by forgiveness and confession, but by careful talking and listening in an attempt to understand each other. It is always wise to be the one to initiate this conversation.

Exercise 2 – Paint a picture

Paint a picture or make a collage based on **Genesis 3.8-24**, entitled 'The consequences of sin'. Plan to bring the finished picture to the group at the end of the week.

You could base your picture entirely on the consequences described in the passage, but you may wish to think more widely than that. The Bible does not teach that every bad thing that happens to an individual is the result of that individual's sin, but it does make a clear link between human sin and human suffering. So your picture could include things like earthquakes, war, mental illness, or accidents.

Try to build into your picture a note of hope. The Bible is awesome in its condemnation of sin and its description of the consequences of sin, and yet we never lose the sense that behind it all is the good and loving purpose of a God who wants the best for us and has good plans for our future.

Exercise 3 – Learn to meditate

Each day, take some time to reflect on the key verses from the first two sessions: **Psalm 23.6** and **Romans 6.23**.

First memorise the verses. Make sure you can recite them accurately just before you go to sleep, and then do the same again when you wake up. If you do this every day for 6 weeks, you will find that you never forget them. And you will find that they are having a profound influence on your life.

Merely memorising verses can become tedious. The way to avoid this is to not only memorise the verses but also meditate on them. You will find that meditating on verses is extremely rewarding.

To meditate on something simply means to think deeply about it. All of us meditate all the time – it is just that some meditation is unhealthy and some is healthy. An example of unhealthy meditation is watching a pornographic film. Worrying is another very common form of unhealthy meditation.

The trick is to meditate only about good things. There are many good things in life that are worthy of our thinking time; the key verses are just one example. This week meditate on **Psalm 23.6** and **Romans 6.23** whenever you can and, as the course continues, meditate on the verses which come in the remaining sessions. Meditate on these verses whenever you are walking on your own, or whenever you are waiting for someone to arrive or for an event to start. Meditate in bed and in the bath; meditate sometimes instead of watching television.

One way to meditate effectively is to think about the verse one word at a time. Begin with the word 'surely' in Psalm 23.6. What does the verse say that you can be absolutely sure about? Think about it for a while then reflect on the word 'goodness'. What does it mean to say that God is good to you? Have you experienced God's goodness today? And so on.

As you meditate you may become aware that God, the Holy Spirit, is speaking to you. You will know this when any of the following start to happen:

- It feels as if a light is going on in your head as you begin to understand something that you have never properly understood before.

- Your emotions are affected so that you feel happy or sad, peaceful, wistful, remorseful, or hopeful.

- You find yourself resolved on a new course of action, perhaps to make a change in the way that you are living.

- You find yourself praying, talking back to God as you realise that he is talking to you.

Before you meditate, ask that this may happen – that you will indeed begin to hear the voice of God. Keep it up, and by the end of the course you will be in a completely new place with God.

Exercise 4 – Preparation for Session 3

In the next session we shall be thinking about Jesus, and as a result some of us will probably change our views about him. As you prepare for the session ask yourself 'What are my views about Jesus now? Who do I think he was? And how firmly do I hold that view? How open am I to changing my ideas about Jesus?'

Many centuries ago, the Church came up with some clear statements of what it is that Christians believe. These statements of belief are called creeds. Have a look at this section of the Nicene Creed, which talks about Jesus:

We believe in one Lord, Jesus Christ,
the only Son of God,
eternally begotten of the Father,
God from God, Light from light,
true God from true God,
begotten, not made,
of one Being with the Father.
Through him all things were made.
For us and for our Salvation
he came down from heaven;
by the power of the Holy Spirit
he became incarnate of the Virgin Mary,
and was made man.
For our sake he was crucified under Pontius Pilate;
he suffered death and was buried.
On the third day he rose again
in accordance with the scriptures;
he ascended into heaven
and is seated at the right hand of the Father.
He will come again in glory to judge the living and the dead,
and his kingdom will have no end.

Take some time to read this through and reflect on the words. Is this what you believe about Jesus? Use highlighter pens to indicate the statements that you agree with and understand, and a different colour for those you are not sure about.

Beyond Ourselves

Session 3: Who is Jesus?

Summary of the session

> Jesus was a real man who lived on the earth just like all of us, but the writers of the New Testament present Jesus to us as more than a man. They claim that Jesus was 100% man and also 100% God.
>
> This view of Jesus was not shared by all who met him, and it is not shared by everyone today. But a powerful case can still be made for adopting the New Testament view of Jesus.
>
> The reasons given in the New Testament to believe in Jesus include his amazing ability to perform miracles, his own claim to divinity, his remarkable moral teaching, and his sinless life.
>
> Christians believe that the key to understanding everything – life, death, God, ourselves, the past, the future, suffering, power and authority – is Jesus.

Key verse

John 1:12 – 'But to all who received him, who believed in his name, he gave power to become children of God.'

Exercises following Session 3

Please complete one of these four exercises before you come to the next session; choose whichever one seems best for you. If you have time, you may wish to complete all four. The first three are aimed at helping you to explore what you learned in the first session. The fourth is a preparation for the next session.

Exercise 1 – Jesus – either a madman or the Son of God

Look at this quotation from C S Lewis's classic book *Mere Christianity:*

'People often say this about Jesus: "I'm ready to accept Jesus as a great moral teacher, but I don't accept his claim to be God." That is the one thing we must not say. A man who was merely a man and said the sort of things Jesus said would not be a great moral teacher. He would either be a lunatic - on the level with the man who says he is a poached egg - or else he would be the Devil of Hell. You must make your choice. Either this man was, and is, the Son of God: or else a madman or something worse. You can shut Him up for a fool, you can spit at Him and kill Him as a demon; or you can fall at his feet and call Him Lord and God. But let us not come with any patronizing nonsense about his being a great human teacher. He has not left that open to us. He did not intend to.'

The world's great moral teachers, people like Gandhi or Mandela, have always been modest about themselves, but here, taken from John's gospel, are some of things Jesus said about himself:

- **John 6.35** – 'I am the bread of life; he who comes to me will never go hungry.'

- **John 8.12** – 'I am the light of the world; he who follows me will never walk in darkness.'

- **John 10.9** – 'I am the gate; whoever enters through me will be saved.'

- **John 10.11** – 'I am the good shepherd; I lay down my life for the sheep.'

- **John 11.25** – 'I am the resurrection and the life; he who believes in me will live even though he dies.'

- **John 14.6** – 'I am the way, and the truth, and the life; no one comes to the Father except through me.'

- **John 15.1** – 'I am the true vine. You are the branches. No branch can bear fruit by itself; it must remain in the vine. Neither can you bear fruit unless you remain in me.'

As C S Lewis points out, these things that Jesus said

about himself are either completely true or extreme vanity. Eventually we have to decide for ourselves. Will we choose to believe in Jesus or will we dismiss him completely?

Look at each of the verses listed above and imagine that you are reading them as a believer. For you these are the things Jesus said about himself and so they must be true. Ask yourself:

- How does Jesus want you to respond to each of these statements which he made about himself?
- What will happen if you do make this response?

Exercise 2 – Songs about Jesus

Muslims regard the Koran as the infallible word of God. Mohammed is revered as the prophet through whom the word of God was given, but in other respects Mohammed is an ordinary man. Muslims do not believe that he was divine or that he lived a perfect life.

Christians do not think about the Bible in the way that Muslims think about the Koran, and they do not think about Jesus in the way that Muslims think about Mohammed.

The central claim of Christianity is not that the Bible is the word of God, but that Jesus is the word of God. Everything he said and did during his lifetime, and everything he is saying and doing now, are God's word to this world. Christians do not worship the Bible – they worship Jesus.

Christians do not worship the Bible but they do revere it. Christians revere the New Testament because of what it tells us about Jesus, and they revere the Old Testament because Jesus himself took it so seriously.

So the Christian focus is on Jesus and, because Jesus is so much at the centre of their faith, Christians have often written poems or songs which speak directly to him – often in words of praise and worship. Look at **Philippians 2.5-10** and **Colossians 1 15-20**, both of which are early Christian songs. If you are a musician, try setting one of these songs to music ; or try turning them into lyrics which could be set to music. The early Christians must have sung these songs again and again.

There are lots of excellent songs about Jesus which have been written in recent times, and lots of great songs (or hymns) which were written in the 18th and 19th centuries. You can download such songs from the internet (google 'download worship songs for free'), or you can buy CDs from any Christian bookshop. So this week get hold of some songs about Jesus, play them to yourself, and try singing them over and over again.

Here are some outstanding ones to look out for, but of course there are many more, and new ones are being written all the time.

- All my days (Stuart Townsend)
- When I survey the wondrous cross (Isaac Watts 1707)
- Jesus, lover of my soul (Paul Oakley)
- Crown Him with many crowns (Matthew Bridges 1851)
- From Heaven you came (The Servant King) (Graham Kendrick 1983)
- We want to see Jesus lifted high (Doug Horley)
- Thine be the Glory, risen conquering Son (originally written by Swiss hymn writer Edmund Louis Budry (1854-1932) and translated by Richard Birch Hoyle)
- Jesus, Jesus, Holy and anointed One (John Barnett, Vineyard)
- My Jesus, my Saviour (Michael W Smith)
- Oh for a thousand tongues to sing (Charles Wesley 1739)
- My lips will praise you (Noel & Tricia Richards 1991)

Exercise 3 – Praying in the name of Jesus

This is something which Jesus said to his disciples just before he died:

"Until now you have not asked for anything in my name. Ask and you will receive, so that your joy may be complete" – **John 16.24**.

And this is something which he said just after he was raised from the dead:

"All authority in heaven and earth has been given to me" – **Matthew 28.18.**

Christians believe that Jesus is alive now and has authority over all things. Because he allows us to use his authority, Christians find that if they ask for things in his name they are given what they ask. This is what happened for the disciples after the resurrection. They began to pray in the name of Jesus, and things happened for them just as Jesus said they would.

These are some of things that you can pray for in Jesus' name. Choose one of them and pray every day until something happens. At the next group meeting tell the group what you have been praying for and what happened as a result. You can pray for:

- Peace – not for peace in general terms, but for the peace of God to be given to you personally.
- Forgiveness for anything that you have done wrong. Pray that you will know deep down that you are forgiven.
- Help to overcome any temptation. Just pray in the name of Jesus and claim his authority over whatever is tempting you.
- Healing for yourself or for any of your friends who are asking you to pray for them.
- Wisdom – for a clear sense of what to do in a tricky situation.
- Safety – in travel or in any situation of danger.
- Help with any genuine need that you have, for example if you lack food or friends, or a job or a partner in life.
- Financial needs – though this prayer will only be answered if you yourself are a generous person.
- The gift of the Holy Spirit – though in asking for the Holy Spirit you must first commit yourself to follow Jesus.

Don't forget to pray in the name of Jesus. For example pray 'Father, in the name of Jesus I ask you to give me peace.'

Exercise 4 – Preparation for Session 4

Have a careful look at John chapter 9. There are a number of theories that could be advanced to explain how this remarkable story came to be written. Look at the story and try to decide which of the following theories is most plausible. Bring your conclusions to the next session.

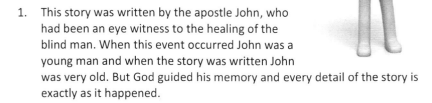

1. This story was written by the apostle John, who had been an eye witness to the healing of the blind man. When this event occurred John was a young man and when the story was written John was very old. But God guided his memory and every detail of the story is exactly as it happened.

2. The story was written after the death of the apostle John by someone who had often heard John tell the story. The story is based on a real incident, the healing of a blind man, but it is arranged to make a point about the blindness of those who do not believe in Jesus; and so the detail of the story is not necessarily reliable.

3. The writer of this story was not an eye witness and was not the apostle John. The writer knew the reputation of Jesus as a healer and believed that this must have been the kind of thing that happened. So although the story is not strictly true the writer is inventing an example of the kind of thing that did happen.

4. This story was written about seventy years after the death of Jesus, when the Christian church was quite well established. The writer of this story has reasons of his own for wanting to persuade people to believe in Jesus. So this story, like the whole of John's gospel, is an invention which the writer hopes will persuade people to throw in their lot with the Christians. It is only loosely based on facts.

What do you think?

Beyond Ourselves

Session 4: Is there life after death?

Summary of the session

Christians believe what Jesus believed and taught: that there is life after death. This belief puts suffering into perspective, because this life and all we do in it is merely preparation for something more significant.

Christians base their belief in life after death on the stories found in the New Testament about the resurrection of Jesus.

The claim that Jesus is alive is made in four separate accounts which tell of many different occasions on which he was seen alive after his death.

The New Testament stories which we read today can be shown to be the same as the original stories written two thousand years ago. These stories contain eye-witness accounts from people who could not have been mistaken and had no motivation to lie.

The story of the resurrection is further confirmed by St Paul in a remarkable letter in which he outlines the evidence that had persuaded him to believe that Jesus was still alive.

After the resurrection many people who had not seen Jesus with their own eyes nevertheless came into a spiritual relationship with him. Jesus by his spirit was alive in them, and the same is true today.

Although the truth about Jesus' resurrection is based on very strong evidence, it cannot be proved scientifically. Belief in Jesus requires us to have faith.

Faith is commitment to something we believe to be true but can't prove. In practice faith in Jesus always brings rewards – rewards that those who lack faith do not share.

Key verse

John 3.16 – 'For God so loved the world that he gave his only Son, so that everyone who believes in him may not perish but may have eternal life.'

Exercises following Session 4

Please complete one of these four exercises before you come to the next session; choose whichever one seems best for you. If you have time, you may wish to complete all four. The first three are aimed at helping you to explore what you learned in the first session. The fourth is a preparation for the next session.

Exercise 1 – Write a sketch about the future

Write a short sketch in which there are two characters. The sketch is set somewhere in the afterlife – about a hundred years after these two people have died, left the earth and gone to heaven.

One of the characters had an easy life on earth. She lived to be a hundred, never had a day's illness, had a huge and happy family, and was never short of money. The other character was born with a deformity and lived a short life in great pain.

The point of your sketch is for the two characters to discuss their former lives, and in particular to consider which of the two had been the more fortunate. Before you start, first ask yourself what points can be made in favour of one or the other of these lives being the one to prefer?

If you are pleased with your sketch, bring it along to the next session. The group may like to perform some of the sketches!

Exercise 2 – How reliable are our memories?

Choose a couple who you know who have been married to each other for a long time and ask them if they will help you.

Interview each of them independently so that neither knows what the other is saying to you. Ask each to give you an account of the early days of their relationship from when they met until the honeymoon.

Make careful notes and write up each account. Notice the things about which the two accounts agree and also the places where there are discrepancies. Then feedback your findings to the couple.

Now look at **Luke 1.1-4** and **John 20.30-31**. You can see the serious intention of both gospel writers to tell you the truth. But how much of what Luke and John wrote is likely to be accurate?

Finally look at **Matthew 20.29-34** and **Luke 18.35-43**, and think about the accuracy of these two accounts. For example did the incident happen on the way into Jericho or on the way out? Do you think there was one blind beggar or two? And do you think one of them was called Bartimaus?

What are your conclusions? Do you think a blind beggar (or two) was healed outside Jericho? Or do you think Matthew and Luke have both made up the same story? Or what?

Now ask yourself, do you think that Jesus was seen alive after he had died?

Exercise 3 – What if the resurrection was true?

Roger was a vicar in Corby in Northamptonshire, where he made friends with a businessman called Ian. Ian would often enquire politely about Roger's work and this would sometimes lead into a conversation about the Christian faith. Ian was always pleasant but always unpersuaded. As they parted Roger would often say 'One of these days, Ian, you must give me an hour of your time and let me show you the evidence that persuades me of the truth of Christianity.'

One day Ian surprised Roger by saying he was up for it. They met, and Roger went painstakingly through what the Bible said about the resurrection of Jesus. At first Ian was cool and polite, but as the evidence mounted he suddenly sat bolt upright and said 'This has to be true!' 'Yes, I think it does,' said Roger.

'Then that means,' said Ian, 'that my friends and I who spend most of our days hitting little white balls around golf courses are actually wasting our lives!' 'I am afraid it may,' said Roger, knowing that he had got through and that his friend was about to make a radical change in the way that he lived.

In this true story, Ian realised that if the resurrection really happened this would mean a big change in the way he was living. What about you? If you really believed in the resurrection of Jesus, what difference would it make to your everyday life? Before you answer, look up the following verses from the Bible: **Matthew 5.27-30, Luke 6.22-23, 1 Corinthians 15.30-34, 1 Corinthians 15.58,** and **2 Timothy 4.7-8.**

Exercise 4 – Preparation for Session 5

This Sunday, go to a communion service (often called a Eucharist) at a nearby church and, if you are invited to do so, join in with the eating of bread and the drinking of wine. Before you go, read **Mark 14.12-26**, which is the story of what happened on the night before Jesus was crucified. He ate supper with his friends (often called the Last Supper) and instituted what we now call the communion service or eucharist. When you go to church, watch carefully how the service is conducted.

To fully understand the eucharist it helps to know a bit of background. In Old Testament times, the Jews made sacrifices for sin. This is how it worked:

First an animal was killed and its blood poured into a bowl. Then the priest would go into the holy place and offer the blood as a sacrifice to God. The priest went on behalf of the people, hoping that the blood which he offered would be an acceptable sacrifice, one that would satisfy the wrath of God and so cause God to turn away his anger from the people. Because the people sinned repeatedly, this sacrifice had to be repeated again and again. The people had sinned and deserved to die, but the animals died in their place.

Christians believe that in much the same way when Jesus died on the cross he was offering up his own blood as a sacrifice for our sins, not only for the sins of the Jews but for the sins of the whole world. This sacrifice was made once and for all – it did not have to be repeated. When Jesus died on the cross he was both the sacrifice for sin and also the priest who offered that sacrifice.

In many churches you will see this being acted out. Look carefully and you will see the sacrifice of Jesus portrayed in the eucharist. A modern day priest, often wearing robes, represents Jesus. This priest offers up the bread and the wine, which symbolise the body and blood of Jesus.

In other Christian churches you will find that there is no ritual offering up a sacrifice to God. Instead the bread and wine which represent Jesus are offered to the people as spiritual food. Notice if this is what happens at the service to which you go.

Reflect on what you see and bring your reflections to the group when you next meet.

Beyond Ourselves

Session 5: The death of Jesus

Summary of the session

> Jesus died by crucifixion after false accusations and a rigged trial.
>
> Jesus died because God loves us.
>
> The death of Jesus was an expression of God's forgiveness, not only for those who killed him but for all mankind.
>
> The death of Jesus was an example. Those who follow Jesus are committed to forgiving all those who have harmed them.
>
> The death of Jesus was a satisfaction of the law of God. God's justice demands that those who sin (break God's law) must die. But Jesus died in our place – he died as our substitute.
>
> The death of Jesus was a victory over all evil spiritual powers and established the final authority of Jesus over all things.
>
> Jesus could have avoided death. He died as an act of submission out of love for his Father.

Key verse

1 Peter 3.18 – 'For Christ also suffered for sins once for all, the righteous for the unrighteous, in order to bring you to God. He was put to death in the flesh, but made alive in the spirit.'

Needed for use during Session 5

During session 5 you will be asked to look at this summary of a true story about forgiveness told by Catherine Marshall.[1]

Harvey and Jack were fellow students at university. Jack seemed without friends and so Harvey, concerned for him, suggested that the two of them should share a flat together. Jack moved in, but his behaviour grew worse and worse, with many outbursts of anger and much heavy drinking. Harvey, who was a Christian, decided to move out and leave the flat to Jack.

Harvey told Jack of his decision. Jack pleaded with Harvey not to go, but Harvey was firm. At this Jack flew into a rage and attacked Harvey with a knife. Twice the knife plunged into Harvey's chest. Jack stood horrified as the blood stains spread on Harvey's clothes. 'Harvey I am so sorry – can you forgive me?' By this time Harvey's mind was in a haze. But he heard himself say 'Yes, Jack, of course I forgive you.' And then he lost consciousness.

Harvey survived the surgery, but only just. He had been in the theatre for eight hours. Afterwards he lay on his hospital bed, his life in the balance and very afraid. And all the time he was thinking about Jack. Was he really willing to forgive him? His emotions said 'no'. All he could feel was a surging resentment and a mountain of self pity. As these feelings grew, Harvey realised that forgiveness is much harder than he had thought. 'Help me, God,' he prayed over and over.

Harvey was praying for the ability to forgive Jack because he knew that Jesus had forgiven him. At last Harvey found the strength to forgive, and he prayed 'Father, forgive Jack. I do not want you to hold what he has done against him. Father I want you to bless him.' At last Harvey had found peace.

For ten more days Harvey's life was on a knife edge, but then the doctor came to him with good news: 'You are going to get well. I am quite confident now.' 'All thanks to you,' said Harvey. 'No,' the doctor said, 'It's because of you. I have watched you closely for ten days and I have noticed how you have been at peace within yourself. If you had held on to any hate at all, that negative emotion would have sapped so much of your strength that you would probably have died.' Forgiveness had been hard, but it had saved Harvey's life.

---

[1] *Beyond Ourselves*, Hodder & Stoughton 1998.

Exercises following Session 5

Please complete one of these four exercises before you come to the next session; choose whichever one seems best for you. If you have time, you may wish to complete all four. The first three are aimed at helping you to explore what you learned in the first session. The fourth is a preparation for the next session.

Exercise 1 – Responding to forgiveness

Turn to **Luke 7.36-50** and read the story. The woman realised that Jesus had forgiven her sins and she responded extravagantly – so extravagantly that some people were offended.

Sometimes in life we find that another person has loved us far beyond what we have deserved. Perhaps this person showed us exceptional kindness beyond the call of duty. Perhaps they accepted us as their friend when we knew we were not worthy of such a friendship. Perhaps they overlooked our faults and weaknesses when those faults and weaknesses were only too obvious to us. Perhaps they made sacrifices for us, or did things for us that went far beyond their responsibilities. Perhaps they brought us into their home or looked after us when we were in trouble.

Make a list of the people in your life who have treated you in any of these ways, so much so that they left their mark on you. How do you feel about these people now? How would you like to respond to them?

Now think about Jesus hanging on the cross, dying for your sins, suffering in your place and praying for you as he died. How do you respond to this? Are you like the woman in the story? Does his death for you make you want to act extravagantly?

The woman in the story loved Jesus and she showed it in her own particular way. How could you show your love for Jesus?

Exercise 2 – Feeling bad?

This exercise is about handling our negative emotions. The three primary negative emotions which trouble all of us from time to time are guilt, fear and anger.

These three emotions are built into the way we are made and are vitally necessary for our welfare. If we did not feel guilty when we did something wrong, there would be no restraint on the way we behave. If we were to be in grave danger yet feel no fear, then we would probably take one risk too many and come to harm. If we were to be badly treated and yet feel no anger then we would probably never learn to defend ourselves, and would become ready victims.

In practice most people experience one of these three emotions more than they do the other two. What about you – do you most often experience guilt, fear or anger? Choose one of the three to consider further.

Sometimes these negative emotions play tricks on us. Sometimes we feel guilt when we have really done nothing wrong at all; fear when there is no danger; or anger against someone who meant us no harm. This is when negative emotions can become unhealthy. If you are suffering a lot from unhealthy emotions then you would be wise to seek out an experienced minister or counsellor who will help you to understand the origin of your emotions and deal with them. So before you go on, check up that there is a real basis for the emotion that you are feeling.

The rest of this exercise assumes that the negative emotion you have chosen has a genuine cause – in other words, that it is a healthy emotion. If you feel guilty, it is because you have done something wrong. If you feel afraid, this is because there is something to fear. If you are angry, it is with good reason.

1. If your problem is guilt, look first at **Psalm 103.12**:

> 'As far as the east is from the west,
> so far he removes our transgressions from us.'

Take a piece of paper and make a list of all the things you feel guilty about. Weight the paper with a stone. Now throw the stone as far away from you as you can. If you live near water throw it out into the water and watch it sink. If you live near a hill go to the top and throw it down. Now feel the distance God has made between you and your sins. The Bible teaches that the cross is the means by which Jesus removes our guilt far from us.

2. If your problem is fear, look up **Psalm 23.6** and **Romans 8.32**. Write them out at the top of a large piece of paper:

> 'Surely goodness and mercy shall follow me all the days of my life, and I shall dwell in the house of the Lord my whole life long.'

> 'He who did not withhold his own Son, but gave him up for all of us, will he not with him also give us everything else?'

On the rest of the piece of paper write down your fears. Make a list of all the things which you fear may happen.

Now cut out a paper cross and place it on the same piece of paper. Meditate on the cross and on the two scriptures. God has given his Son for you. This must mean that God loves you very much indeed. So do you think that the plans he has for you are good ones or bad ones? If God is in charge of your life, what reason do you have to fear?

3. If your problem is anger then look at **Mark 11.25**:

> 'Whenever you stand praying, forgive, if you have anything against anyone; so that your Father in heaven may also forgive you your trespasses.'

Make a list of all the people you have something against, noting down what it is you have against them.

Now look at **Luke 23.34** and see how Jesus prayed for the people who had put him on the cross. Speak out loud and ask God to forgive each of the people on your list. Thank God that he does not hold your sins against you; ask him not to hold the sins of the people on your list against them.

Exercise 3 – Overcoming evil

In this exercise we take some first steps in spiritual warfare. You may prefer to do this exercise together with a friend, especially if the idea of spiritual warfare seems strange.

First turn to **1 Peter 5.8-9**:

'Discipline yourselves; keep alert. Like a roaring lion your adversary the devil prowls around, looking for someone to devour. Resist him, steadfast in your faith, for you know that your brothers and sisters throughout the world are undergoing the same kinds of suffering.'

Jesus lived in a constant battle with Satan, his enemy. We saw in the session that the enemy was finally defeated on the cross. When Peter tells us to resist Satan, he knows that we can resist him successfully – so long as we do it in the name of Jesus.

Here are three areas in which you may be able to use the power of the cross to resist Satan.

1. **Habitual sins.** If you have habitual sins that you just cannot get on top of, it is probably Satan who has brought this bondage into your life. Identify any habitual sins that are spoiling your life. Satan wishes you to keep on doing these things. Jesus wishes you to be rid of them. The cross shows us that Jesus is stronger than Satan.

2. **Negative thoughts** – things which are not true but which Satan likes to tell you are true! Here are some examples of negative thoughts which many people have and which you may also be having:

- I am too bad to ever be fully forgiven.
- God answers the prayers of others but he will never answer one of mine.
- I am an inferior person – that is the way I was made.
- People are not to be trusted so I should be very careful.
- The future is probably bad.
- The more I please people the more they will like me.
- Strong people don't ask for help.
- My childhood will always affect me.
- I should never upset anyone.
- I need to be sure in order to take decisions

All these things are untrue. Satan wishes you to continue to believe that they are true because that way he can make you fearful, angry or guilty. Jesus wants you to stop believing these things and start believing the opposite so that you may have freedom. And Jesus is stronger than Satan.

3. **Frequent setbacks**. Sometimes God allows suffering to enter our lives and uses the suffering to strengthen our faith. But a lot of the negative stuff in life does not come from God – it comes directly from Satan. So if you meet a succession of setbacks don't put up with it; resist Satan in the name of Jesus. Jesus wants these things to stop happening to you, and the cross demonstrates that Jesus is stronger than Satan.

Resist Satan by saying this prayer. Say it every day until there is a change:

'Heavenly Father, I believe that Jesus won a victory over Satan on the cross and that his power is greater than Satan's power. Here Lord, are some of things that I am always doing wrong... I ask you that these things may stop, and I resist Satan in Jesus' name. Here Lord, are some of my negative thoughts... I renounce these negative thoughts and declare that they are lies. In the name of Jesus I say to you Satan that you may no longer trouble me in this way. Finally Lord I claim your protection against all the things that are going wrong in my life and I pray in the name of Jesus that they will stop.'

Say this prayer out loud. If you have never done this before it will seem quite strange – but go ahead and do it and you will see the power of the cross at work in your life.

Exercise 4 – Preparation for Session 6

Here are five things which we have learned about Jesus during the last two sessions. Look carefully at each one.

- Jesus was both fully human and fully divine. He is unique and special, totally different from any human being that has ever lived.

- Jesus overcame death and is still alive.

- Jesus came to this world so that human beings could be forgiven for all their sins and so be reconciled to God.

- Jesus paid a terrible price on the cross; he did this entirely because God loves us.

- Jesus now has complete authority over every kind of evil.

These statements are either absolutely true, pure gold; or they are utterly false. What do you think?

Try suspending any doubts you may have about the truth of these statements. For a moment, decide to believe them. Go over each of the five things one by one and think 'Now that I really believe that, how does it make me feel, and what difference will it make to my life?'

Beyond Ourselves

Session 6: How to become a Christian

Summary of the session

> It is possible to become a Christian by sincerely saying a simple prayer of commitment.
>
> A Christian is someone who believes in Jesus and resolves to trust him about all the big issues of life. The prayer of commitment expresses this faith.
>
> A Christian is someone who has received from Jesus. In the prayer of commitment we become children of God, we ask for forgiveness of our sins, we ask for the gift of the Holy Spirit, and we ask for the gift of eternal life.
>
> A Christian is someone who has made a decision to follow Jesus. In the prayer of commitment we resolve to live by his priorities and to turn away from everything which we know to be wrong or evil.

Key verse

Acts 2.38 – Peter said to them, 'Repent, and be baptized every one of you in the name of Jesus Christ so that your sins may be forgiven; and you will receive the gift of the Holy Spirit.

Needed for use in Session 6

Here are six possible definitions of a Christian based on the key verses from the first six sessions:

Acts 2.38 – Christians are people who have repented and been baptised; their sins have been forgiven and they have received the Holy Spirit.

Psalm 23.6 – Christians are people who are experiencing God's love on a daily basis and are confident that this will go on forever.

Romans 6.23 – Christians are people who have received the gift of eternal life from Jesus although they have not earned it.

John 1:12 – Christians are people who have welcomed Jesus and as a result have found that God has become a personal father.

John 3.16 – Christians are people who believe in Jesus and who, by believing, have received eternal life.

1 Peter 3.18 – Christians are people who have come to God having been set free from sin through the death of Jesus.

Later in the session you will be asked to look at the following exercise. One way of defining a Christian is to say that a Christian is someone who has made a decision; the following verses each describe that decision. Look at them all carefully and then try to say what this decision is. What is it that all followers of Jesus have decided to do?

Mark 1.15 – 'The time is fulfilled, and the kingdom of God has come near; repent, and believe in the good news.'

Matthew 4.19 – 'And he said to them, "Follow me, and I will make you fish for people."'

Acts 2.38 – 'Peter said to them, "Repent, and be baptized every one of you in the name of Jesus Christ so that your sins may be forgiven; and you will receive the gift of the Holy Spirit."'

Luke 14.26-27 – 'Whoever comes to me and does not hate father and mother, wife and children, brothers and sisters, yes, and even life itself, cannot be my disciple. Whoever does not carry the cross and follow me cannot be my disciple.'

Matthew 13.44 – 'The kingdom of heaven is like treasure hidden in a field, which someone found and hid; then in his joy he goes and sells all that he has and buys that field.'

Matthew 7.13-14 – 'Enter through the narrow gate; for the gate is wide and the road is easy that leads to destruction, and there are many who take it. For the gate is narrow and the road is hard that leads to life, and there are few who find it.'

Prayer of commitment to Jesus – there will be an opportunity for you to say the following prayer during this session:

'Lord Jesus, I believe in you. I believe you lived as a man. I believe you died for my sins on the cross. I believe you rose again from the dead. I believe you are alive now.

'Lord Jesus, I put my trust in you. I trust that your death is sufficient for all my sins. I trust in you that you will take me through all the difficulties of my life and bring me safely to a place with you in heaven. I trust in your instructions for my life. I will try to live by your priorities. I will be unashamed of you to my friends. I will not willingly do wrong.

'Lord I open my heart to you and pray that you will send to me the gift of the Holy Spirit."

Exercises following Session 6

Please complete one or more of these exercises before you come to the next session.

Exercise 1 – What to do now

This exercise is especially for those who have recently prayed the commitment prayer.

First look at this verse from **2 Corinthians 5.17** – 'If anyone is in Christ, there is a new creation: everything old has passed away; see everything has become new!'

According to this verse, if you prayed the prayer you are now a new person. You have told Jesus that you will follow him for the rest of your life and that you will live by trust in him. And you have asked him to come and live in you. Life is going to be very different from now on.

40

Jesus will be in your life. And God, the Father of Jesus, has become your Father too.

There are two things to do now. The first is to tell someone what you have done. Anyone will do really, but perhaps the best is to think of someone you love and who loves you. Don't worry at all about how they will react; just go to them and say that you would like to share something very important that has just happened to you.

The second thing to do is to start to read the Bible every day. You have begun a new life, and you will need food to sustain it. The Bible will act as spiritual food.

- Set aside 15 minutes every day to read the Bible; make these 15 minutes as early in the day as possible. Before breakfast is usually best.

- Start with Mark's gospel and read about ten verses each day.

- Before you start reading, thank God that you are now a new creation and that God's Spirit lives in you. And ask him to speak to you as you read.

- Then read the passage very slowly, thinking about the words one at a time.

- When you have finished reading, write a prayer. The prayer should be partly about what you have read, but also make one request – one thing that you would like your Father God to do for you today.

Exercise 2 – Putting Jesus first

This exercise is a prayer exercise for you to do on your own with God.

Turn to **Luke 14.26**. Jesus uses the very strong word 'hate', which at first sight puts us off. How can I be expected to hate my father and mother, my wife and my children, when actually I love them all very much?

Actually Jesus is just being very dramatic in order to make his point and grab our attention. We might have expected him to say that if we want to follow him we have to hate bad things, like greed or violence or lust. That would be easy to understand. But Jesus knows that it is not the bad things in our lives that will keep us from putting him first. It is the good things, like our homes, our families, our careers, our money.

Make a list of all the good things in your life, the things on which you place the most value. For example you might list the people you love, a job you enjoy, a possession you cherish, or a hobby that engrosses you. In the prayer exercise you will offer all these things to Jesus. You will say to Jesus that you do not wish these things to be more important to you than he is.

Kneel down and raise your hands in front of you with the palms flat and open. Then imagine that you are placing all the items on your list on your open hands and offering them to Jesus. As you do, say a prayer – aloud.

For example suppose you are a father with a daughter whom you love very much indeed. Make a prayer similar to the one below. In this prayer you are handing over responsibility for your daughter to God. Once the prayer is made, Jesus has the ultimate responsibility for what happens to your little girl – but because he loves her and he loves you, you have no need to fear.

'Jesus I love my little girl, but I want to learn to love you even more than I love her. So Jesus I give her to you. She is not mine, she is yours, and I ask you to take charge of her and to take care of her. I thank you so much that I am able to keep her and look after her, but as I do so I will often look to you for guidance and help. I know that one day I will be parted from her. I hope that will not be for a long time but I will leave that decision to you and I will trust you. I thank you Jesus that I will never be separated from you and neither will she. While she remains in my care may she also rest in your care.'

Say a similar prayer for each item on your list, and finally offer your whole self to Jesus, remembering his promise that he will always be with you whatever the circumstances.

Exercise 3 – Giving and receiving

Consider **Luke 6.38**, where Jesus is teaching an important principle. The Christian life works by giving and receiving. This exercise is one to attempt for a whole week, 24 hours a day, 7 days a week.

Spend the whole of this week in giving; try to make sure you miss no opportunity. Give money, presents, a helping hand, a smile, a word of encouragement: give everything you can think of, and give to each person you meet. Do not let a person go until they have received something from you.

Each time you give something to someone else, turn to Jesus and ask him to give something to you. Here are some of the things for which you might ask.

- **John 14.27** – 'Peace I leave with you; my peace I give to you. I do not give to you as the world gives. Do not let your hearts be troubled, and do not let them be afraid.'
  Jesus promises peace. If you need peace, ask for it. He loves to give you his peace.

- **Matthew 6.**8- 'Your Father knows what you need before you ask him. **John 16.24** – 'Until now you have not asked for anything in my name. Ask and you will receive, so that your joy may be complete.'
  Jesus loves to give you what you ask for. So ask him for what you need.

- **1 John 1.9** – 'If we confess our sins, he who is faithful and just will forgive us our sins and cleanse us from all unrighteousness.'
  Jesus has paid the penalty for our sins. He does not wish us to carry guilt around with us. So ask for his forgiveness.

- **1 Corinthians 10.13** – 'No testing has overtaken you that is not common to everyone. God is faithful, and he will not let you be

tested beyond your strength, but with the testing he will also provide the way out so that you may be able to endure it.'
Are you under pressure of any kind? Jesus wants to help you.

- **James 1.5** – 'If any of you is lacking in wisdom, ask God, who gives to all generously and ungrudgingly, and it will be given you'.
Are you unsure of what to do next? Ask him to guide you and listen for his wisdom.

Remember; in this exercise only ask Jesus to give to you **after** you have given to someone else.

Exercise 4 – Preparation for Session 7

Think back over your life and make a list of all the people who have made a big difference to you. These should be people of whom you can honestly say that, had this person had not come into your life, you would be a different person today. In each case try to write down:

- What difference has this person made in your life?
- What was so special about them?

Get in touch with at least one of these people and thank them for what they have done for you.

Next think about the influence that God has had on your life to this point. What difference, if any, has God made, and how did God do this? Write a prayer thanking God for the different ways in which he has been a part of your life.

Finally look at **Revelation 3.20**: 'Listen! I am standing at the door, knocking; if you hear my voice and open the door, I will come in to you and eat with you, and you with me.'

This verse gives us a graphic description of how God, the Holy Spirit, can come into our lives. Has this happened to you?

The next session will look at what happens when the Holy Spirit comes.

Beyond Ourselves

Session 7: The Holy Spirit

Summary of the session

> The Holy Spirit is God living in or with a person or group of people.
>
> The Spirit is given by God to people of his choosing, always as an act of grace.
>
> The Spirit was given before Jesus came, but only to a few people; these people were enabled in one way or another to do remarkable things.
>
> The Spirit fell upon Jesus at his baptism; all his miracles were done through the power of the Spirit.
>
> Jesus promised that after he had gone to heaven his Spirit would be given to all who believed in him. This proved to be true.
>
> The first occasion was on the day of Pentecost when a new community was born amongst whom the Spirit lived and worked. There were many things about this community that would not have been possible without the Spirit.
>
> In the same way, the Holy Spirit is available today to all communities of believers, however small.
>
> There are other kinds of spirits, called evil spirits, which can affect our lives negatively; but evil spirits can always be dealt with by prayer in the name of Jesus.

Key verse

Luke 11.13 – 'If you then, who are evil, know how to give good gifts to your children, how much more will the heavenly Father give the Holy Spirit to those who ask him!'

Needed during Session 7

During session 7 we will be looking at some verses which describe the activity of the Holy Spirit from the beginning until the time of Jesus.

Deuteronomy 34.9 – 'Joshua son of Nun was full of the spirit of wisdom, because Moses had laid his hands on him; and the Israelites obeyed him, doing as the Lord had commanded Moses.'

Acts 9.17 – 'So Ananias went and entered the house. He laid his hands on Saul and said, "Brother Saul, the Lord Jesus, who appeared to you on your way here, has sent me so that you may regain your sight and be filled with the Holy Spirit".'

Matthew 3.16 – 'And when Jesus had been baptized, just as he came up from the water, suddenly the heavens were opened to him and he saw the Spirit of God descending like a dove and alighting on him.'

Matthew 12.28 – 'If it is by the Spirit of God that I cast out demons, then the kingdom of God has come to you.'

Joel 2.28-29 – 'Then afterwards I will pour out my spirit on all flesh; your sons and your daughters shall prophesy, your old men shall dream dreams, and your young men shall see visions. Even on the male and female slaves, in those days, I will pour out my spirit.'

John 7.37-39 – 'On the last day of the festival, the great day, while Jesus was standing there, he cried out, "Let anyone who is thirsty come to me, and let the one who believes in me drink. As the scripture has said, 'Out of the believer's heart shall flow rivers of living water'."Now he said this about the Spirit, which believers in him were to receive.'

Later in session 7 you will be asked to look at this list of things which the Holy Spirit sometimes brings to a person's life when he comes to them. Choose one of these things – something that you long for. Then if you wish it someone will pray for you that you will be given this particular gift.

- The ability to have a two-way personal relationship with God
- The ability to become a better person
- The ability to love other people endlessly

- The ability to love to pray
- The ability to read the Bible with enjoyment and understanding
- The ability to receive God's grace through the sacrament of bread and wine
- The ability to make great sacrifices for others
- The ability to be caught up in the praise and worship of God
- The ability to teach the scriptures to others
- The ability to win others to faith in Christ
- The ability to be wise
- The ability to know things as you pray
- The ability to know what to pray for
- The ability to pray for others to be healed
- The ability to pray for miracles
- The ability to know what God wants to say to a person or a group
- The ability to know whether something is from God or from Satan
- The ability to speak in tongues or understand tongues

Note that this is not an exhaustive list of all that the Holy Spirit can and does do.

Exercises following Session 7

Please complete one (or more) of the following exercises before you come to the next session.

Exercise 1 – The Holy Spirit in the Old Testament

In this week's session you looked at the example of Joshua, one of the first people in the Bible to receive the Spirit. In this exercise you will identify other biblical characters who also received the Spirit. Look up as many of the references as you have time for. In each case ask yourself what the Holy Spirit accomplished through this person.

- **Exodus 35.30-36.1**   Bezalel & Oholiab
- **Numbers 11.16-17/Nehemiah 9.20**   Moses
- **Judges 3.10**   Othniel
- **Judges 6.34-35**   Gideon
- **Judges 11.29**   Jephthah
- **Judges 14.6,19/Judges 15.14 & 15**   Samson
- **1 Samuel 10.6, 9, 10**   Saul
- **1 Samuel 16.12-13**   David
- **2 Kings 2**   Elijah & Elisha
- **Isaiah 48.16**   Isaiah
- **Micah 3.8**   Micah
- **Zechariah 4.6**   Zerubbabel
- **Isaiah 11.1-5, 42.1-7, 61.1-3**   The coming Messiah

Imagine that the Holy Spirit comes to you and starts to work through you (which of course he very well may!). Which of the Old Testament characters in this exercise comes closest to what you would like to see happen in your life?

Exercise 2 – The Holy Spirit in Jesus

In this week's session we saw how the Holy Spirit acted through Jesus to deliver a man from an evil spirit. But this was not the only way in which the Holy Spirit worked through him. Look up these Bible passages to see what happened as Jesus ministered in the power of the Holy Spirit:

- **John 7.14-16**   Jesus had supernatural wisdom
- **Luke 5.4-6**   Jesus had supernatural knowledge
- **John 4.50**   Jesus had extraordinary faith
- **Luke 7.2-10**   Jesus had power to heal
- **Luke 8.29**   Jesus had authority over evil spirits
- **John 6.11**   Jesus performed miracles
- **Matthew 24.1-35**   Jesus was a prophet who was able to see into the future
- **John 2.24-25**   Jesus discerned what was in a man's heart
- **Luke 4.18**   Jesus was anointed to preach good news

Today Jesus lives on earth by living in the church, that is, he lives in Christian communities of all sorts, large or small. God's plan is that no single Christian should be able to do all the things which Jesus did, even if that single Christian is full of the Holy Spirit. Instead God's plan is that each church should together be like Jesus. So between them the people in the church will have supernatural wisdom, supernatural knowledge, and so on.

This means that the Holy Spirit wants to work through you as well as through the other people in your church or in your group. The way he uses you is not up to you – it is up to him. But the Spirit will not mind if you speak to him and ask him for a particular gift. So have a think and a pray – what is the desire of your heart? Would you like to be the one whom the Spirit uses to provide wisdom, or knowledge, or faith, or healing, or authority over evil spirits, or miracles, or prophecy, or discernment, or anointed preaching? Talk to the Holy Spirit about this.

Exercise 3 – Thinking again

Reflect again on the key verse from Session 6, **Acts 2.38**: 'Peter said to them, "Repent, and be baptized every one of you in the name of Jesus Christ so that your sins may be forgiven; and you will receive the gift of the Holy Spirit."'

Peter told the crowd in Jerusalem that if they were to receive the Spirit they must first repent. The word repent means literally 'think again.' A revolution must occur in the mind. You used to think one way — now you need now to think in a completely different way.

The people in Jerusalem were challenged to think again about Jesus. Six weeks earlier these same people had demanded that he be crucified as if he was a common criminal. But when Peter spoke to them on the day of Pentecost, they realised that Jesus was the Son of God raised from the dead. So you too think again about Jesus. What did you think about him before? How did you treat him? What do you think about Jesus now, and how will you treat him now?

You have changed the way you think about Jesus. Now change your thinking about today. How do you usually think about a day? What is it for? How will you use it? Now you are a Christian, a follower of Jesus, 'think again' about today:

- Are you expecting goodness and mercy to follow you today?
- When you are in trouble today, who will you look to for help?
- When you are alone today, who will you turn to?
- By what moral standards will you live today?
- What kinds of words will come out of your mouth today?
- What opportunities will you have today to give to others?
- When people treat you badly today, how will you react?
- Who will be encouraged today because you encouraged them?
- With whom will you share some truth about God today?
- Who will you pray for today?

Now that you have repented (thought again), ask for the gift of the Holy Spirit to fill you up for the day ahead, so that you become a different person in the way that you live today.

Towards the end of the week write to a friend explaining how your thinking is changing as a result of doing this course. Tell your friend how you are trying to make room in your life for God to fill you with his Spirit.

Exercise 4 – Preparation for Session 8

In this week's session we saw how Joshua was described as being 'full of the Spirit'. Turn to **Ephesians 5.18** where Paul advises 'do not be full of wine but be full of the Spirit.' In this exercise we are going to think about what it means to be full.

Make a point of noticing whenever something is full. Examples you might notice are a bus or a train full of passengers, a football ground full of supporters, a glass full of water. This week take every opportunity you can to fill things. Fill your briefcase, eat until you are full, fill a drawer to overflowing, fill a pillowcase with a pillow. Fill your lungs with air. Fill a room with the sound of music.

As you observe these things, reflect on the difference between something being full and something being half full or empty. And each time you look at something to see if it is full, ask yourself what it would be like to be full of the Holy Spirit.

If you are good at drawing paint a picture whose title is 'Being full'.

In **Romans 5.5** Paul talks about the Holy Spirit being poured into the hearts of believers. In **Luke 11.13** Jesus says that this will happen to you too if you ask him. So ask and ask! Make up your mind not to be content with a Christian experience which is like a half-full glass.

Beyond Ourselves

Session 8: Receiving the Spirit

Summary of the session

The Holy Spirit is given to any believer who asks for him. It often happens that the Spirit comes as other believers lay hands on a person and pray in the name of Jesus.

The gift of the Holy Spirit is given as a guarantee of the promise of eternal life. The Holy Spirit's presence always has tangible results.

One result of the Holy Spirit's presence is that those who have the Spirit find themselves in a new relationship with God. They find that the love of God has been poured into their hearts. They are called God's children.

Those who have the Spirit gradually change under the Spirit's influence so that bad things drop away and good things appear.

Those who have the Spirit find that the Spirit speaks to them. The Spirit teaches, the Spirit guides, the Spirit encourages, the Spirit rebukes.

Those who have the Spirit find that they are drawn into a Spirit-filled community along with others who also possess the Spirit.

Key verse

John 7.37-39 – 'Let anyone who is thirsty come to me, and let the one who believes in me drink. As the scripture has said, "Out of the believer's heart shall flow rivers of living water." Now he said this about the Spirit, which believers in him were to receive.'

Needed during Session 8

During Session 8 you will need the words of this song by Michael W Smith:

> This is the air I breathe
> This is the air I breathe
> Your holy presence
> Living in me
>
> This is my daily bread
> This is my daily bread
> Your very word
> Spoken to me
>
> And I... I'm desperate for you
> And I... I'm lost without you...

Exercises following Session 8

Please complete one (or more) of these exercises before you come to the next session.

Exercise 1 – Draw close to God

You will find that now you have the Holy Spirit you will have begun to have a relationship with God. You love God and you are finding that God loves you. God is now your father, and you are his child.

As with any relationship, if this new relationship is to be a success, it must be maintained. It takes effort to maintain a relationship. God has promised to do his part, as any good father would, but the relationship is still going to take effort on your part. Even if you do not make any effort, God will not go away. He will still be there, and he will still love you and make lots of efforts to gain your attention, just as a human father would. Nevertheless, the more you draw near to him, listen to him, learn from him and serve him, the more you will experience the reality of his care.

Begin to set aside a time each day to be quiet in the presence of God and, if possible, make this quiet time the first thing you do every day. Find a place where you will not be interrupted.

There are no rules about the length of time that you should give to this, but if it is to be of real value you will need at least 15 minutes. You could use the time to repeat any of the exercises in this book. Exercise 1 from session 6, or exercise 3 from session 7 would be particularly appropriate.

An alternative is to devote the time to the key verses which you have been learning. Each day, meditate carefully on as many of the verses as you have time for. Ask the Holy Spirit to speak to you through the verses and respond by talking to him. Talk to him also about the events of the day ahead. Ask for his help with anything that might prove difficult and his guidance over anything that seems at all confusing.

Keep this up on a daily basis and you will be amazed by how much you will change, and how much you will come to know and love God personally.

Exercise 2 – Find a friend

This is another way to make an effort in your new relationship with God. Plan to spend an evening this week in the company of a Christian friend. Choose someone who you feel has clearly received the Holy Spirit. Ask this person if it would be all right for you to spend an evening together reading the Bible and praying.

When you meet, start by looking together at a story from the Old Testament. A good place to start is with the story of Jonah. Read the first chapter, talk about it and pray together. If praying seems a bit odd to you don't worry about it – it is quite easy and you will get used to it. When you pray, just open your mouth and talk to God as if he were in the room with you, and you will soon find that he really is in the room with you! When you pray with someone else it is best to pray aloud. When your friend is praying just listen to the prayer and carry it to God with him or her.

After some time in the Old Testament, switch to the New Testament and to the story of Jesus. A good place to start is with John's gospel, so read **John 1.1-18**. Once you have finished reading, sit in silence together and meditate carefully on the passage. Then share what you have been thinking about and what you think God is saying to you. Then pray together.

Finally, look together at a Psalm. **Psalm 23** is a good choice. Read the Psalm aloud together, reflect on it, and then pray. You may find that you both want to carry on with these sessions – so next time look at Jonah chapter 2, the next bit of John, and a different Psalm.

End by thinking ahead about the issues and decisions of both your lives and bring these issues to God in prayer.

Exercise 3 – Entering into heaven

Turn to **Acts 13.1-3**. In this story a group of Christians in Antioch decided they would go without food and instead they spent their time in worshipping God, and asking him to guide them about the future. God did guide them, and as a result a great missionary work began.

So this week choose one meal to miss, and instead of eating spend the time worshipping God. Look at **Revelation chapter 4** where the apostle John describes his vision of heaven. In your imagination go through the open door (verse 1) and ask that the Spirit of God will come through that door with you (verse 2). Picture the throne (verses 2-3) and worship God. How will you worship him? It is up to you! Will you be silent, speak, shout, clap or play music? Will you kneel, sit, stand, or will you prostrate yourself before the throne? Whatever you do, take your time. Do not move on until the Spirit has made you fully aware of how awesome God is.

Now that you are aware of God, it is time to realise something else. You are a child of God. This awesome God is your Father, and this makes you a prince or a princess in heaven. In your imagination approach the throne, receive the embrace of your Father and sit at his feet. How does this feel?

Now, from your vantage point sitting at your Father's feet, look slowly through verses 4-11 and absorb each element of the picture. Finally join in the worship of verse 11 and repeat the words to yourself over and over again.

Then think about your life and its direction. What decisions do you have to make? What direction are you supposed to go in? Ask God to speak to you.

Did you find that going without food helped you to concentrate?

Exercise 4 – Preparation for Session 9

Session 9 will be about God's promises to us and our promises to God.

To prepare for this, make a list of your most important human relationships. What promises have you made to each of these other people, and what promises have they made to you? In some relationships these promises will have been written down or spoken out – for example in a marriage ceremony. In other relationships the promises have never been spelt out but are nevertheless real, for example the commitment a parent feels towards a child.

As you think about your relationships you will probably see that, in some cases at least, the other person is being consistently faithful to what they have promised to you. Make this a cause for rejoicing, because the happiness of our lives depends on there being people on whom we can rely. Perhaps it would be a good idea to thank these people for their faithfulness to you.

You will probably also see that some of these important people in your life show a high degree of trust in you. Once again rejoice and be amazed at your good fortune. You know yourself, and you know that you are not 100% reliable. But isn't it good that there are some people in your life who always seem to trust you and always seem to overlook your faults and mistakes?

But not all relationships work well. Is there someone in your life who has not been faithful, perhaps conspicuously so? Could you overlook this and continue to trust them? Or has trust broken down more or less completely? Is there anything that you can do about it?

Are there some of your relationships in which you yourself have not been completely faithful? You did not keep your promise. You let the other person down. You did not fulfil your responsibilities. If so, make an opportunity to apologise, ask forgiveness, and then renew your commitment.

Successful relationships depend on trust as well as on faithfulness. Is there someone in your life who does not trust you? If so, is there anything you can do to regain that person's trust? Or does the fact that they do not trust you say more about them than it does about you?

Do you think that the people on your list believe that you trust them? What could you do to demonstrate that you do?
Pray for the people on your list, and especially about those relationships that are not going well. Ask the Spirit to give you wisdom to know what to do next.

Beyond Ourselves

Session 9: God's promises

Summary of the session

A relationship with God depends on promises – ours and God's.

The Christian life succeeds as we are faithful to our promises and trust in God's promises.

God promises that as we trust in Christ all our sins, past, present and future, are forgiven.

God promises that once we have put our trust in Christ he will be like a father to us. He will never give up on us and will be with us even in life's most difficult moments.

God promises that after death we will live with him eternally.

It is up to us to trust that God will keep his promises. This should not be difficult as these promises are guaranteed by the presence of the Spirit in our lives.

Key verse

2 Peter 1.4 – 'Thus he has given us, through these things, his precious and very great promises, so that through them you may escape from the corruption that is in the world because of lust, and may become participants in the divine nature.'

Needed during Session 9

The promises of God

During Session 9 we will look at the subject of God's promises.

You will be asked to look at the following Bible passages and consider these questions:

1. What, in a nutshell, is the promise God is making to us in these three passages?

2. What difference will it make to our lives if we maintain our trust in this promise?

- **Psalm 103.10-12** – 'He does not deal with us according to our sins, nor repay us according to our iniquities. For as the heavens are high above the earth, so great is his steadfast love towards those who fear him; as far as the east is from the west, so far he removes our transgressions from us.'

- **1 Peter 3.18**– 'For Christ also suffered for sins once for all, the righteous for the unrighteous, in order to bring you to God. He was put to death in the flesh, but made alive in the spirit.'

- **1 John 1.7-9** – 'But if we walk in the light as he himself is in the light, we have fellowship with one another, and the blood of Jesus his Son cleanses us from all sin. If we say that we have no sin, we deceive ourselves, and the truth is not in us. If we confess our sins, he who is faithful and just will forgive us our sins and cleanse us from all unrighteousness.'

Once you have identified the promise contained in these three passages you will be asked to look at two further passages, which contain a different promise, and to answer the same questions: What is the promise, and what will happen to us if we trust it?

- **John 10.27-29** – 'My sheep hear my voice. I know them, and they follow me. I give them eternal life, and they will never perish. No one will snatch them out of my hand. What my Father has given me is greater than all else, and no one can snatch it out of the Father's hand.'

- **Romans 8.31-39** – 'What then are we to say about these things? If God is for us, who is against us? He who did not withhold his own Son, but gave him up for all of us, will he not with him also give us everything else? Who will bring any charge against God's elect? It is God who justifies. Who is to condemn? It is Christ Jesus, who died, yes, who was raised, who is at the right hand of God, who indeed intercedes for us. Who will separate us from the love of Christ? Will hardship, or distress, or persecution, or famine, or nakedness, or peril, or sword? As it is written, "For your sake we are being killed all day long; we are accounted as sheep to be slaughtered." No, in all these things we are more than conquerors through him who loved us. For I am convinced that neither death, nor life, nor angels, nor rulers, nor things present, nor things to come, nor powers, nor height, nor depth, nor anything else in all creation, will be able to separate us from the love of God in Christ Jesus our Lord.'

Then finally you will be given two more passages which contain a third promise. Once again your task is to answer the same questions. What is the promise, and what difference will it make to us?

- **John 14.1-6** – 'Do not let your hearts be troubled. Believe in God, believe also in me. In my Father's house there are many dwelling-places. If it were not so, would I have told you that I go to prepare a place for you? And if I go and prepare a place for you, I will come again and will take you to myself, so that where I am, there you may be also. And you know the way to the place where I am going.' Thomas said to him, 'Lord, we do not know where you are going. How can we know the way?' Jesus said to him, 'I am the way, and the truth, and the life. No one comes to the Father except through me.'

- **Philippians 1.21-23** – 'For to me, living is Christ and dying is gain. If I am to live in the flesh, that means fruitful labour for me; and I do not know which I prefer. I am hard pressed between the two: my desire is to depart and be with Christ, for that is far better.'

Signs of the Holy Spirit's presence

Later in the session you will need this list of the signs of the Holy Spirit's presence in our lives. You will be asked to look at the list to see if any of these things have been happening in you:

- a new peace
- a new happiness
- a new awareness of when we are doing wrong
- a special love for other Christians
- a new desire to do good
- answers to prayers
- a desire to tell others about Jesus
- finding that the Bible, especially the verses we are learning, is speaking to us

A final prayer

At the end of the session the group will say the following prayer together.

'Father God, we speak to you today to affirm our trust in the promises which you have made to us. First, we thank you Father that, because Jesus has died for us on the cross, we can be sure that all our sins have been forgiven and forgotten by you. We promise to forgive ourselves, to forget about the past, and to move on with our lives, looking forward to what you have planned for us.

'Father, we thank you for your promise that nothing can ever separate us from your love. Thank you that through our faith in Jesus we have come into your family. We are now your children and, through the presence of the Holy Spirit in our lives, we experience your love every day. We promise that we will expect good things from you and that when they come we will acknowledge you and thank you.

'Father, we thank you that even when hard things happen in our lives your love still surrounds us. We thank you that you know us, you love us, and that you always have a plan. We promise that whatever happens we will trust you and continue to praise you.

'Father, we thank you for your promise of eternal life. We promise to think often about the great reward that is ahead of us. We thank you that Jesus was faithful to you even to the point of death and that he now reigns with you in glory. We thank you that Jesus promised that what happened to him will also happen to us and we promise that as he was faithful so will we be.

'Father, we thank you that Jesus made it completely clear how his disciples were to live. We have decided to be his disciples and to live by his priorities. We promise to study his teaching carefully and to apply it diligently to our lives.

'Father, we want to tell you that we have turned our backs on sin. If you show us that something is wrong we are resolved not to do it. When we find that temptation is strong, or that we are weak, we will always seek your help. We want to be those who overcome and not those who are defeated.

'Father, our loyalty to Jesus is absolute. We love him, we worship him. He is our God as you are our God. We will always honour him and always hope to speak of him to others. It will be our greatest delight and dearest hope to lead others to believe in him and to know him for themselves.'

Exercises following Session 9

Please complete one (or more) of these exercises before you come to the next session; choose whichever one seems best for you.

Exercise 1 – Meditation

You have now become familiar with nine key verses and will perhaps have committed them to memory. Each night this week before you go to sleep, and again each morning as you wake, see if you can remember them.

It is meditating on these verses that will bring rewards. Each day take every opportunity to meditate for a few minutes on the nine verses. Good times to do this are when you travel alone, when you go for a walk and when you have to wait for the next thing to happen. Before you begin to meditate, remind yourself that the Holy Spirit is now with you and that he will speak to you as you meditate. When you hear the Spirit's voice, respond in prayer.

A good way to meditate is to think about one word at a time. Say the verse, putting an emphasis on just one word and then thinking and praying about that word. Then move on to the next word.

If you are able to sit down for your meditation time, find a piece of paper and a pen and draw a picture or a diagram which incorporates, or tries to incorporate, every idea that the verse contains.

Another way to meditate on a verse is to write it out in your own words – but try to use only 10 words for each verse. For example this week's verse, **2 Peter 1.4**, has 34 words. Try rewriting it in 10 words, without losing any of the meaning. One possibility might be 'change from corruption to godliness comes by trusting God's promises.' Can you improve on this?

Exercise 2 – Giving thanks

Try this exercise at the beginning (or end) of each day. The exercise is based on **Ephesians 5.20**, which says 'always giving thanks to God the Father for everything, in the name of our Lord Jesus Christ.'

If you are doing this at the end of the day, make a list of six good things that have happened today. If you are doing it at the beginning of the day think of six good things that happened yesterday. You will find that there always are six good things, but it may take you a little time to think what they were. Keep going until you have a list of six – you will often find that it is the sixth item that makes you smile and realise how good God is. When the list is made, thank God for each item on the list.

Thanking God for everything means thanking him for the bad things that happen as well as the good things. Christians thank God for the bad things because of our faith in the promise that nothing can separate us from the love of God. Suppose for example that you have just missed the last train home. The circumstances are not good. On the face of it the choice is between an expensive taxi or a long wait for the early morning train. The wise thing to do if you are a Christian is to take your eyes off the problem and concentrate on the fact that God loves you. These circumstances offer you an opportunity to hand your life over to God and to once again prove that all things work together for good for those who love him (see **Romans 8.28**). In time you will be able to see the good that God is able to bring out of this situation.

After you have made your list of six good things, write down one bad thing that has happened today and bring that to God too, thanking him for his love for you even in this situation. You will find that the bad thing is much easier to remember, except that on some days there will be no bad things at all.

Thanking him for the six good things is rewarding because it will remind you of how much your life has been blessed. Thanking him as you recall the one bad thing serves a different purpose. The experience of pain tests our faith and helps us to draw closer to God (see **James 1.2-4**). So say to God 'Thank you so much for this opportunity to grow in my faith. Once again I choose to trust you, to believe that you are present in all the circumstances of my life, and that you love me.'

If you think about it, the ratio of six good things to one bad thing is just about right. Seven bad things would be too hard, but if we had seven good things our faith in God would never be tested and we would not become strong.

Exercise 3 – Learning to love

Think about a key relationship in your life. If you are married, choose your marriage partner. If not, choose someone else with whom you have close ties. In the session you considered how relationships are based on promises, spoken or unspoken. Relationships work if each party does their best both to be faithful to the promises they have made and also to trust the other, always giving them the benefit of any doubt there may be.

In most key relationships the essence of the promise made is a promise to love and to keep on loving. In marriage, for example, each says to the other 'I promise to love you no matter what, and to love you forever.'

So this exercise is based on **1 Corinthians 13**, Paul's great chapter on love. The nature of love is described in detail in verses 4-7, and summarised by verse 7: 'Love bears all things, believes all things, endures all things, hopes all things.'

- 'Love **bears** all things.' Think about your relationship with the person you have chosen. Are you happy to accept this person exactly as they are, or are there things about them that you are always trying to change? First reflect that God accepts *you* exactly as you are. This is part of what God means when he says to you 'I love you'. He does not say 'When you change, then I will love you'.

  Note that although we should accept each other's weaknesses and each other's annoying side, we should not accept each other's sinful behaviour any more than God accepts ours. Sinful behaviour in a close friend should always be instantly forgiven and instantly challenged. This is part of loving someone and being faithful to them.

- 'Love **believes** all things.' Are you trusting this person, believing in the goodness of their intentions towards you, or are you suspicious, worried, doubtful? Reflect that God is disposed to trust you. He believes in your commitment to him. He has enormous belief in your potential to do good. God is delighted that he has entered into a relationship with you, and is hugely optimistic about that relationship. Are you trying to adopt the same attitude?

On occasions it is sadly true that trusts break down. Just as God has to conclude sometimes that a person whom he has loved has turned away from him so sometimes do we. But we should not reach this conclusion easily.

- 'Love **endures** all things.' No one is perfect, and there will have been times when this person has behaved badly towards you. Have these times been forgiven and put behind you; or do they still rankle in your memory? Reflect that God has forgotten every mistake that you have made. He has expunged it from his memory. Could you perhaps do the same?

- 'Love **hopes** all things.' How do you view the future of your relationship? Do you believe that the best is yet to come; or are you resigned to the relationship's mediocrity? Reflect that God has not given up on you. He is working hard to make the future of your relationship with him much better than the past.

If your relationship has lost some of its spark, try your hardest to reignite it. Perhaps you could return to some of the places and activities which you associate with a time when your love was strong. Perhaps you could take the initiative and plan an exciting holiday. Perhaps you could spend some money on a present. Perhaps you could look at yourself in the mirror and do something to smarten yourself up.

Exercise 4 – Preparation for Session 10

This exercise is based on the story of Thomas in **John 20.24-29**. Ask yourself what it was that Thomas was having doubts about? And what was it that resolved his doubts?

Now ask yourself, 'When I am at my lowest, what doubts do I have about the Christian faith?' For example do you ever think that:

- The story of Jesus we have in the Bible may be untrue
- God does not love you

- After death God will just forget you
- God does not exist at all

What would it take to resolve your doubts? Jesus resolved Thomas' doubts by providing the evidence that what he doubted was in fact true. What evidence is there that the things that *you* have doubted are in fact true? What additional evidence do you need? Perhaps Jesus will provide you with this evidence, as he did for Thomas. Why don't you speak to Jesus and ask him?

Having doubts is not wrong; indeed it is perfectly natural. God understands this and will not abandon us just because we have doubts. But doubting does not help us; it leads nowhere and it brings no rewards. Jesus said to Thomas that although he had provided him with evidence, it would have been better if he had believed without the need for further evidence.

The thing that does always bring rewards is faith. Consider **Hebrews 11.6**, which makes this clear. Once we have decided to put our trust in Jesus we always find that Jesus rewards our faith by making himself known to us in one way or another. At some point each of us has to decide to stop doubting and believe. There is no other way forward.

Do you think you could just decide to believe that God is there, that he loves you, that he has revealed himself to you in Jesus, and that through Jesus he has given you the gift of eternal life? If you are happy to just believe these things, then why don't you tell God so? Speak to him with all your heart and thank him for what he has done.

Beyond Ourselves

Session 10: Living by faith

Summary of the session

When we first come to Christ:

- We promise to turn from our sins and try to live by his teaching and example
- We promise that we will never deny him but will devote our energies to his cause.
- We come always as an act of trust in his promises to us – promises of forgiveness, unending care, and eternal life.

We continue our relationship with Christ by maintaining our trust in what has been promised to us and by continuing to be faithful to what we have promised to him.

The way to remain faithful is to continually set our minds on the things of the Spirit. If we do this then the Spirit's power will keep us faithful.

Even so, faithfulness on our part is hard to maintain. When we fail we find ourselves in a spiritual battle. Satan will accuse us and tell us that because of our failure God has ceased to love us. We must not listen to this voice. God has promised to keep us and God always keeps his promises.

Unfaithfulness on our part should be immediately confessed, forgiveness should be received, and the relationship restored. This forgiveness is guaranteed by the cross

Just as faithfulness is hard to maintain, so is trust hard to maintain. Many doubts will enter our minds and threaten to undermine our trust.

Doubt is not a sin, but it is an enemy to faith. Faith always brings rewards but doubt brings no rewards.

Doubt is resolved by revisiting the evidence for our belief, and then by renewed commitment to our promises.

Key verse

Hebrews 11.6 – 'And without faith it is impossible to please God, for whoever would approach him must believe that he exists and that he rewards those who seek him.'

Needed during Session 10

Here are some of the ways in which you can choose to set your mind on the things of the Spirit.

- Enjoying creation, the things which God has made
- Meditating on the key verses that have been part of this course
- Having a time of quiet in the morning for reflection and prayer
- Going to church
- Coming to the group meeting
- Singing hymns and spiritual songs
- Reading the Bible
- Listening to CDs of sermons or spiritual music
- Listening to the Spirit and being obedient to his voice
- Any of the things listed in **Philippians 4.8**

During session 10 you will also need this prayer which the group will be asked to say together.

'Father, we admit that sometimes we doubt you. We doubt that you exist. We doubt that you love us. We doubt that you have forgiven us. We doubt that you will answer our prayers. We doubt the promise of eternal life.

'Father, we are sorry that we sometimes doubt you. We are like Thomas who doubted even though all the evidence was there for him to believe. We thank you Jesus for the gracious way you dealt with Thomas, and we ask you to be gracious to us.

'We acknowledge that these doubts originate in our spiritual enemy Satan. In the name of Jesus we cut ourselves off from him and claim your protection. As Jesus prayed, so we pray 'Father, keep us from the evil one.'

'Father, we know that we can only please you if we will believe in you. So we commit ourselves once again to being believers, people who will put our trust in you and wait for you to respond. We look for you to reward us once again by giving us your Spirit.'

Exercises following Session 10

Please complete one (or more) of the first three exercises given below.

Exercise 1

In this course we have concentrated on ten key verses. Each of these verses can be used by the Holy Spirit to keep us on track.

Here are ten life situations. Each describes a Christian who is going through a hard time. Look at each one and ask yourself which of the verses would be of help to these ten people.

- Arthur surveys the wreck of his life. Arthur is 56 but he feels as if his health has gone forever. He has little money and little prospect of ever having any, and he knows that this is his own fault. Drink has been his problem and he fears that it always will be.

- Bill is a dutiful man who tries hard to be good. But his over-sensitive conscience troubles him. He lives in a perpetual state of guilt.

- Alice sits in church and feels like an outsider. The church is full of people who appear to be in love with God but Alice knows that she isn't, and she wonders if she ever will be.

- Richard is having a frustrating day. When he came home he lashed out in anger at his wife, who is not a Christian and who responded: 'If you really were a Christian, Richard, you would not have done that.'

This message is coming to Richard not only from his wife but also from his own heart.

- Mary is lonely and has no friends. She has a job which she does dutifully but finds boring. Today is Christmas Day, and once again Mary is spending Christmas on her own.

- Jane has found a lump in her breast and fears that this may mean cancer. Jane is afraid of death.

- George is full of doubts. He has been reading Richard Dawkins and is impressed with some of his arguments. But George knows that he does not wish to give up his faith.

- John's beloved wife has died and it is the day of the funeral. His wife was very sure that she was going to be with God – but as John sits in the church and looks at the coffin, he is not so sure.

- Margaret is a vicar. She loves the people in her church but can see that their religion is very shallow. She longs for them to have an experience of God that will change their lives.

- Kelly is a teenager who has become a Christian but is having a hard time at home. Her father is the problem. Her brother is his favourite, and he has always been very sarcastic with Kelly. Now that she has become a Christian things are worse than ever.

Which of these ten people is most like you and which of the key verses do you need most?

Exercise 2 – Praying about the hard things in life

This exercise is best done at bedtime. Make a list of all the things that have gone wrong today – anything that has hurt you, upset you or made you feel bad. The idea is to not go to bed until these things have been put to rest.

Divide your list into three. Begin with those

things that you know were your fault. Turn to **1 John 1.9** and on the basis of this promise write or put together a prayer in which you confess the day's sins and failures to God. Now turn to **Hebrews 10.17** and ask yourself what has happened to your sins as far as God is concerned.

Secondly, consider the things that went wrong because of what somebody else did. Turn to **Mark 11.25** and see that whatever and whoever it is, you must forgive. So compose another prayer acknowledging your pain and asking your Father in Heaven to forgive each person who has made today difficult for you.

The third list consists of those things which just happened – which seem, in a way, to be God's fault. Turn to **Romans 8.31-39** and put together a third prayer. In this prayer, express your resolve that although the events of today have tested your faith, you still choose to believe that God loves you and he is in charge of the events of your life.

Exercise 3 – In the hand of God

Look at **John 10:27-30** and try to imagine what happened as Jesus was teaching.

First look at verse 28. Can you see Jesus holding out one of his hands and asking each member of his audience to imagine themselves being held by him. Then Jesus closes his hand, saying 'No one can snatch you out of my hand.'

Now look at verse 29. Can you imagine Jesus holding out the other hand, also flat? Jesus says 'This hand is my Father's hand. Then imagine Jesus closing this hand too and saying 'No one can snatch you out of the Father's hand.'

Now look at verse 30 and imagine Jesus clenching together the two hands and saying 'I and the Father are one.'

Now do you feel safe? Repeat the exercise several times during the week, especially if times are difficult.

If you have time, read **Psalm 139** slowly and carefully. Reflect on all that this Psalm reveals about God – that he is all seeing, all knowing, all powerful, and present everywhere. Reflect on how he knows everything about you and understands you even in those situations where you don't understand yourself. Think about the security of being in the loving hand of God who knows you completely and still accepts you and loves you.

Now look at **John 14.27**. Do you see that Jesus wants to give you peace? Bow your head and ask him for his peace. Then, if you have the skills, paint a picture based on this verse. Plan to give your picture to a friend who needs the peace of Jesus.

Exercise 4 – Looking ahead

We hope that working through *Beyond Ourselves* has been rewarding, and that it has helped you to grow in your relationship with God. Now it is time to seriously consider what you will do next. If you have enjoyed *Beyond Ourselves*, why not move on now to Book 2 of the series, which is called *The New Community*? If you do plan to do this, here is an exercise to get you started.

Session 1 of Book 2 is about baptism, and baptism is an example of what is called a joining ceremony. In baptism a person joins the family of God, both the visible form which is the church of God on earth, and the invisible form which is the church of God in heaven. In baptism a person is born again of the Sprit of God. In baptism a person's sins are washed away. In baptism a person commits to a lifelong faith in Jesus.

Think of the joining ceremonies which you have witnessed or been part of. For example, did you ever join the brownies or the cubs?

Ask yourself what was meaningful about these joining ceremonies? Did they help the people involved to realize that they had joined something and that life had changed?

Think about the marriage service, probably the most common of all joining ceremonies. At a marriage service, what transaction is taking place and how does the use of symbolic actions help those present to realize the significance of that transaction?

- What promises are made and by whom?
- What assurances about the future are given to those making the transaction?
- What assurances about the past are given?
- Who should be present at the ceremony?
- What clothing is appropriate? What music? What readings? And is it good to have a talk or speeches?

Apply these same questions to the ceremony of baptism.

Key verses

Psalm 23.6 – 'Surely goodness and mercy shall follow me all the days of my life, and I shall dwell in the house of the LORD my whole life long.'

Romans 6.23 – 'For the wages of sin is death, but the free gift of God is eternal life in Christ Jesus our Lord.'

John 1:12 – 'But to all who received him, who believed in his name, he gave power to become children of God.'

John 3.16 – 'For God so loved the world that he gave his only Son, so that everyone who believes in him may not perish but may have eternal life.'

1 Peter 3.18 – 'For Christ also suffered for sins once for all, the righteous for the unrighteous, in order to bring you to God. He was put to death in the flesh, but made alive in the spirit.'

Acts 2.38 – 'Peter said to them, 'Repent, and be baptized every one of you in the name of Jesus Christ so that your sins may be forgiven; and you will receive the gift of the Holy Spirit.'

Luke 11.13 – 'If you then, who are evil, know how to give good gifts to your children, how much more will the heavenly Father give the Holy Spirit to those who ask him!'

John 7.37-39 – 'Let anyone who is thirsty come to me, and let the one who believes in me drink. As the scripture has said, "Out of the believer's heart shall flow rivers of living water." 'Now he said this about the Spirit, which believers in him were to receive.'

2 Peter 1.4 – 'He has given us, through these things, his precious and very great promises, so that through them you may escape from the corruption that is in the world because of lust, and may become participants in the divine nature.'

Hebrews 11.6 – 'And without faith it is impossible to please God, for whoever would approach him must believe that he exists and that he rewards those who seek him.'